MW01352136

Mary, Mother of All

Mary, Mother of All

Scott Hahn & Emily Stimpson Chapman

Illustrated by Tricia Dugat

Steubenville, Ohio
www.emmausroad.org

Emmaus Road Publishing
1468 Parkview Circle
Steubenville, Ohio 43952

Printed in Canada

ISBN: 978-1-64585-262-9 Hardcover | 978-1-64585-263-6 Ebook
Library of Congress Control Number: 2022945098

Cover design and layout by Tricia Dugat

To our (twenty-one) beloved grandchildren. —S.H.

For Toby, Becket, and Ellie. Fly to her always. —E.C.

Once upon a late summer morn,
a brave young girl named Mary was born.
Conceived without sin, strong and true,
Mary had work God made her to do.

Called to be mother, queen, and bride,
called to help save us from deadly pride.
Through her, God planned the world to bless.
But first, young Mary had to say yes.

Yes to a plan made long ago;
Yes to the love to which Eve said No;
Yes to suffering, tears, and pain;
Yes to her loss, and yes to our gain.

This plan was born when angels fell
and made their home in a place called hell.
Flung far from God and full of hate,
Satan took aim at man and his mate.

A serpent's form he donned that day,
and told a lie to lead us astray.
Eve, then Adam, the lie believed,
and Satan's sad goal was thus achieved.

Death to God's life
within the soul;
Death to bodies
now broken,
not whole;

Death to man's joy
working the land;
Death to the dance
God perfectly planned.

But to all this death,
God said No;
in His love,
He would not let us go.

He'd bless the woman
with His Son,
and Satan's worst work
would be undone.

The patriarchs,
the prophets, too,
waited for One
who'd make all things new.
Judges and kings
of Him were signs,
but what of the woman
in God's design?

The woman who'd bear God's own Son;
The woman who'd make the demons run;
The woman who'd reign by Christ's side;
The woman in whom God would abide.

She’s there in Eve, mother of all,
undoing knots made tight by the Fall.

She's Deb'rah, Esther, Rahab too,
ever defending the faithful few.

She's Israel's ark, hid from strife,
holding God's Word, High Priest, Bread of Life.

Then, at last, she's the king's right hand,
wise Queen Mother helping lead the land.

Mary, most holy, wise, and true;
Mary, these signs are pointing to you;
Mary, God's choice made before time;
Mary, say "yes" and reverse Eve's crime.

To Mary's home in Naz'reth went
the archangel who from God was sent
to bear great tidings, bring great news,
and to find out what Mary would choose.

Would Mary bear a son and a king
who would the wide world's salvation bring?
Would she consent to God's great plan
to help the Son redeem fallen man?

"Yes," she said,
"I am God's handmaid."
"Yes," she said,
"I will be not afraid."

"Yes," she said,
"let God's will be done."
"Yes," she said,
"I will carry the Son."

The angels then sang out with joy,
God Himself would become Mary's boy!
He'd grow and learn, laugh, teach, and pray,
With Mary there each step of the way.

Right to the Cross, she followed Him.
Wept as the light in His eyes grew dim.
Consented to His last request;
as mother of all, she would be blest.

Mother of all in grief and loss;
Mother of all bowed down at the Cross;

Mother of all pierced by a sword;
Mother of all who long for Our Lord.

Still Mary hoped no grave could hold
the One of whom the Scriptures foretold.
Her hope proved right on Easter morn,
when Jesus rose to a world reborn.

But on earth He couldn't remain.
The Kingdom of God was His to reign.

Mary lived on ‘til life was done,
then body and soul went to the Son.

Queen of Heaven, moon under feet;
Queen of Heaven, did dragons defeat;
Queen of Heaven, crowned with the stars;
Queen of Heaven, God's mother and ours.

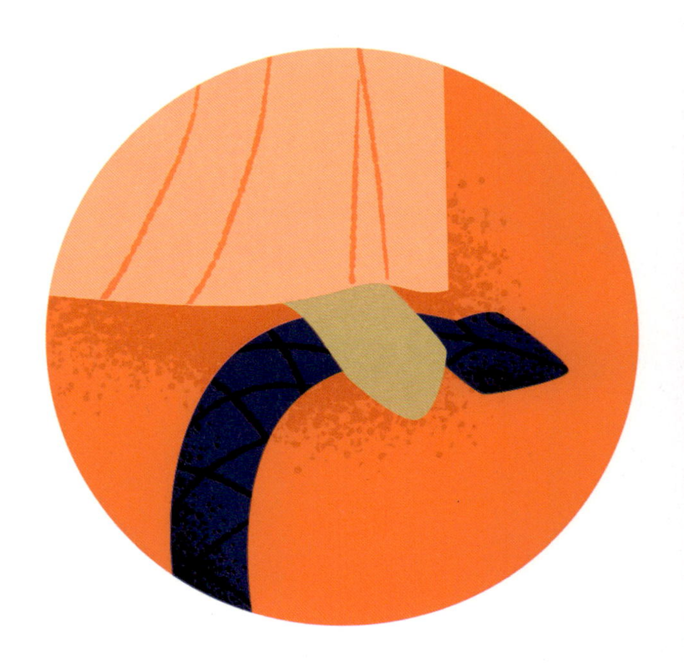

This mama who held Jesus tight,
she holds you too, in your darkest night.

To her you can give every care,
and trust with love your burdens she'll bear.

M
Mama Mary
PRAY FOR US